Of Courage
and
Commitment

Of Courage and Commitment

Carroll Blair

Aveon Publishing Company

ISBN: 978-1-936430-34-5

Library of Congress Control Number
2011904311

Aveon Publishing Co.
P.O. Box 380739
Cambridge, MA 02238-0739 USA

Also by Carroll Blair

Grains of Thought
Facing the Circle
Reel to Real
Shifting Tides
Reaches
Out of Silence
Quarter Notes
By Rays of Light
Into the Inner Life
Gnosis of the Heart
Soul Reflections
Beneath and Beyond the Surface
For Today and Tomorrow
In Meditation
Sightings Along the Journey
Through Desert's Fire
Offerings to Pilgrims
Human Natures
(Of Animal and Spiritual)
Atoms from the Suns of Solitude
Colors of Devotion
Voicings
Through the Shadows
As the World Winds Flow

What does life ask of you,
need from you? . . . . To
raise a spiritual harvest
and deliver it to life.

2

You are alive because there is work
for you to do that has yet to be done.

3

Because you are here you have a right to
be, *but you must still earn your right
to be.*

4

One is born a potential, a possibility, which
may or may not be realized, this realization
the sole responsibility of the individual to
attain or not attain in the course of his life.

5

One's life is one's light, and only as bright
as one has ventured to grow.

6

It is challenge that creates strength, either
in a species or in an individual.

7

A single person could bring down a mountain
with a stone cutter — if he had the years
and patience to do it.

8

One learns so long as one is humble, achieves
so long as one perseveres, grows so long as
one has courage.

9

The nature of a human life is expressed
through the nature of the mind, the heart,
the spirit.

10

Nothing can give of itself all that it was
meant to give until it is fully developed —
and also a human being.

11

Life is ninety-nine percent profound,
one percent superficial, yet many live
as though it were one percent profound,
ninety-nine percent superficial.

12

Should one not reflect daily upon the question: "What am I doing today for the betterment of the world?"

13

To gauge the significance of your journey objectively, reflect on the significance of what you are pursuing.

14

Do not all have a duty to live at the depth
that they are capable of living?

15

Where does one belong in life, where
is one most needed? Wherever one is
(where one can be) at one's best.

16

If you are not doing everything you
are able to do for the benefit of life
you are not doing all that is expected
of you.

17

To withhold your best from the world
is the same as taking something away
from the world.

18

Nothing that comes easily arrives on
the wings of nobility.

19

What good is energy and power without
vision and the cultivation of awareness
and discipline?

20

Discipline is hard, but rich in what is
needed for the progression of spiritual
strength.

21

Whether one has the courage to take
the risk of testing oneself is also one
of life's tests.

22

A body of water must be stirred before it can be known what is beneath it — so too, the essence of a spirit.

23

How many have posed the question to themselves: "What have I to do with life, and what has life to do with me?"

24

Some believe all they need to do is show up
in life and life will take care of the rest.

25

It is what you get used to that uses you up.

26

When one lets himself go he is letting
go of more than just himself.

27

It is not only what one does but what
one doesn't do that is manifests what
one is.

28

People demand much of one another,
but more does life demand from all.

29

What is not earned shall not last
nor can ever be made whole.

30

Subtle is the way of spiritual growth.

31

Profound work begins long before
one realizes that it has begun.

32

One sees not the seed beneath the ground
that brings forth the flower or the fruit.

33

To get to the best that is in you requires
total commitment to the goal of its
realization.

34

Chances are you're doing something that
means something when it is the work and
not the applause that means something
to you.

35

You enter the world with all the powers
of your life, but it is you who must
discover and develop them.

36

The spirit should grow young as the body grows old and does so if one has engaged life with courage.

37

To strive to do more is in itself doing more.

38

If one stops growing how much can one go on as one of the living?

39

Mastery isn't written on a certificate, or diploma, or award, but engraved in the heart of discipline.

40

In every moment of life class is in session.

41

His education is far from advanced who
has never educated himself.

42

A lesson imparted by the wisest sage
cannot penetrate as deeply as a lesson
learned on one's own.

43

One derives more from a puzzle one has
constructed oneself than from one put
together by another.

44

The point of education is missed if it
doesn't inspire you to move beyond
what has been learned.

45

Many things one may teach oneself
who is capable of profound love.

46

To grow in a profound way one must also graduate from oneself.

47

Self-indulgence is self-destruction.

48

Where there is ego one is far removed
from where the highest things are to be
attained.

49

One aspires to nothing of value
until one has learned humility.

50

The noble of spirit work throughout their days to achieve the measure of excellence that the powers of their lives have allowed their best efforts to achieve.

51

Nature's force, ceaseless, without effort, never struggling to sustain itself, unlike the life that it generates, which must strive to sustain and create.

52

No more than one's body can float in the earth's atmosphere can one be raised to a higher state by anyone or anything but the will within.

53

Higher duty is forever calling to all.

54

Every day more is said than thought . . .
more is said than done.

55

A fear of heights is more common in
the spiritual realm than in the physical.

56

The mind and spirit know well of delayed gratification, surrendering the best of their gifts only after great strides have been made in trying to reach them.

57

To live with courage is to strive to be all that one is capable of becoming.

58

One's finest cannot be realized without
freedom from the fear of failure.

59

To acquire something of lasting value
tomorrow you must give all that you
have to today.

60

What is wanted from life beyond the
superficial must first be given to life.

61

No great blessing comes easily into
being.

62

If getting to life's treasures were easy
would they be worth getting to?

63

The better things will always demand the
most sacrifice.

64

You must stay with something firmly
and profoundly before something of
the extraordinary stays with you.

65

Without obstacles to the goal, the goal
would be lost.

66

Intrinsic in every achievement is something
to be employed for the attainment of
further achievement.

67

Wholeness is achieved piece by piece.

68

When you accept the challenges of life
you give yourself (your life) the chance
to *live*.

69

If one has the resolve one can turn
any misfortune into blessing, turn any
tragedy into triumph.

70

Pain is the place that prepares one to
move forward.

71

You benefit much from the sky's rains,
and so too the rains of your life in ways
that you can never know.

72

With each pain endured, with each obstacle overcome, the spirit grows larger, deeper, stronger.

73

Every suffering that is transformed into creative expression bears some spiritual nourishment that may find its way to others.

74

Love is present in every profound
suffering; not so, at every frivolous
pleasure.

75

No tribulation arrives without gifts, but
they are not given at once, and aren't
always recognized or embraced.

76

The things that are hardest for a human
life are the greatest aids to its growth
and transformation.

77

Few have risen to the promise of their
sufferings.

78

One must journey into caverns of darkness
before one can stand in the light of wisdom.

79

Life has as much to teach as one has the
courage to learn.

80

What are they ready to learn, to do
who want of life only to fill their lives
with comfort?

81

Life was never meant to be safe.

82

Truth in all its nature is infinitely more precious than dissimulation and false hopes.

83

All must choose for themselves how much truth they are willing to be part of their lives.

84

To be sheltered from some things is to be
vulnerable to others.

85

Some gloss over their weaknesses and
believe they are building on their strengths.

86

One can hide one's head in the clouds
as well as in the sand.

87

To not face things as they are is to deny
oneself the opportunity to learn from them.

88

All that is false is hollow.

89

Truth is never swayed by compliment
or insult, praise or blame.

90

There is power in the knowledge of
where you are powerless.

91

The ability to accept what life gives to you
in way of burden is a gift — one that opens
the way for other gifts (greater gifts) to
follow.

92

Nothing opens more doors after closing one
than affliction.

93

If an affliction has not been resolved it is
because it has something more to teach you.
(And some afflictions last a lifetime, because
they have a lifetime of lessons to teach.)

94

Sometimes the darkest days produce
the most luminous spiritual light.

95

What despair offers the one who is
despairing is an invitation to move to
something better than anything he or
she is now living or experiencing.

96

If you bear anger because you haven't
had the advantages that others have had,
do you not see what an advantage this
can be . . .

97

If you don't let in the pain you can't
let out the beauty.

98

One can gauge one's spiritual strength by
how much one looks upon one's sufferings
as blessing or curse.

99

You can live with more than you think you
can, and less than you think you can.

100

If the sun lights above the earth each day
can one not rise facing the challenges of
the day, whatever they may be?

101

Even at its most volatile you should never
fear life, for life does not fear itself, and
you are part of life.

102

Flowers are trampled on all the time,
but that doesn't stop them from growing.

103

One who thrives only in states of peace
does not live the fullest or deepest of lives.

104

It is a mistake to assume that harmony
is always absent from discord.

105

The higher picture is ever missed by
those who have never worked the depths.

106

Sometimes one believes that life has
denied him something when in truth
it has spared him a hindrance to what
he needs to develop to realize the
potentials of his life.

107

How many stand by the gravesite
of Was instead of engaging with the
presence of Is.

108

Everyone dies in the present;
not everyone lives in it.

109

The positives of a life that are not
utilized stagnate or atrophy, or
turn into negatives.

110

It is not how busy a life is, but how
concentrated and the focus of its
concentration that determines the
nature of its quality.

111

Many are concerned with the quality of
their lives, but what of the quality their
lives bring to life . . .

112

One cannot go wrong if one seeks the
right things, even if not always found.

113

To be in the service of some things is better
than to be in the command of others.

114

How much sloth there is in much of the world's activities.

115

Growth doesn't always follow change.

116

Because something is the best there is
doesn't mean that it is good enough.

117

There is a difference between the change
that aspires to something higher and more
noble and the one that merely decorates or
rearranges the status quo.

118

How can the highest things be accessible
where ego still lives?

119

The base and the sublime are forever vying
for the soul of man.

120

What a difference there can be between living *the good life* and living a life for the progress of the good.

121

It is the everyday "responsibilities" of life that keep many from confronting their life's responsibility.

122

All growth is work, but not all work
is growth.

123

Who will not examine himself, and
cannot criticize himself, will not
benefit himself.

124

To improve one's life means to improve
oneself.

125

Like all of Nature, one grows from the
inside out.

126

If one's focus is always on the outside
one cannot mature. True maturity is the
province of the inside, developed therein.

127

No wisdom from outside begins to penetrate
until the purgation of inner folly begins.

128

What value can the work possess that is not
rooted in the work that is done on oneself?

129

The most troublesome to others are those
who turn away from doing the inner work.

130

Rare is the virtue that springs from the average nature as naturally and easily as the lilac from its tree.

131

They who cling to ego have no idea how much they would loathe it, how quickly they would set to work to free themselves from it, if they knew how much it was denying them.

132

The final person one stops fooling is oneself.

133

There are many fallacies that can appear
to make things better in the short term,
but not one can do so in the long.

134

Spiritually speaking man rises only to
the degree that the facades of his life
have fallen.

135

A principle is worth only what one is
willing to sacrifice for it.

136

The everyday world is more hostile than
welcoming to virtue.

137

What nothing of the earth can purchase . . .
there is the treasure worth working for,
striving for — worth living and dying for.

138

The real work of a human being must
lead to the spiritual, otherwise one has not
labored as a human being.

139

Spirit — the most generous of entities, but
what must be endured to release its powers
of wisdom and beauty.

140

There is no price tag on what is worth having, but it all comes at a price.

141

Paradise also has its fire.

142

Not only are there joys to be earned,
but also one's sorrows that lead to the
highest of joys.

143

Many gifts lie open to one whose goals
are of the spiritual and pursues them
with a life committed to higher purpose.

144

Some will go anywhere for a piece of gold;
others, for a gleam of light.

145

One can never be rich enough in spirit.

146

The entrance to the spiritual is from the inside.

147

To every station of enlightenment there are properties of the intangible to be taken and others to be left behind.

148

One must not only make the journey
by oneself, one must also clear the way
to the journey.

149

Much in the day-to-day world isn't worth
the effort it demands, but it is worth the
effort demanded to get to where one
needs to be to make this discovery.

150

There are jewels on the surface of life, but it requires inner depth to perceive them.

151

What one learns of the world cannot go beyond a superficial apprehension without a strong sense of self-awareness.

152

What can they know of themselves who are
rarely alone with themselves?

153

He has not begun to know himself who
has not looked into the mirror within.

154

What has he faced with a knowing courage
who refuses to face himself?

155

One must merit the right to be the
navigator of one's life.

156

Their paths are never found who always look to the outside for the answers to their lives.

157

To "be oneself" one has to first discover what one's true self is.

158

Better to get lost on one's own path than to travel safely on the path of another.

159

Hard work is essential to finding one's way, even when not knowing it is being searched for.

160

The inner light doesn't begin to glow until it is discovered.

161

If one is not living near to the essence of one's being, how can one be *living*?

162

One's "I," one's "me," is not one's true self.

163

Who take up the quest for self-realization
come to find that life will help them, but
will not do the work for them, which those
who reach the advanced stages come to
understand and appreciate.

164

To seek treasure only from sources outside
oneself is like begging or borrowing money,
not realizing that there are riches beneath
the ground on which one is standing.

165

What is the gold of the earth compared
to the mines of treasure within, waiting to
be received?

166

Only the misguided forsake their
inner wealth for the sole pursuit of
worldly wealth.

167

All have something inside them worth
more than all there is to see in the
everyday world, but not everyone finds
it, because not everyone goes in search
of it (or even cares to find it).

168

There are thousands of pathways in the mind
and spirit leading to thousands of different
places, yet how many are content to enter not
more than a few, staying in those few places.

169

The spiritual is open to all seekers ready
to discover its truths.

170

One who wears masks is not ready for
the journey of journeys.

171

The spiritual venture is a mystical journey
from deliverance to deliverance.

172

The further one has travelled inside, the
clearer one's perception of the outside.

173

Experience must be taken deeply within
and digested in the tract of inner being,
otherwise its lessons (its nourishments)
lie on the surface unlearned, unused
like good food spoiling, never to be
consumed.

174

What can they know of life, teach of life,
bring to life who have never explored
(never created) the inner depths?

175

The life of the growing spirit is a constant
clearing of the way for new insight and
inspiration to flourish.

176

The work that stands most complete in its
value is the work that proceeds without end.

177

Reverence, gratitude, humility, appreciation
are all closely aligned to wisdom.

178

The wealth of the eternal is always to give, always to serve.

179

To know what is real, what is true, look to what sustains, inspires, transcends.

180

To live in the service of love, truth, beauty
and wisdom is to live no greater life, nor
one more rich in purpose.

181

The optimal life truly is about giving . . .
(and what could they possibly see who
do not see this) . . .

182

Countless offerings are given to those
who make of their lives an offering to Life.

183

To receive from the eternal so you may
give to the world . . .

184

When the body goes what else matters but one's body of work and deeds for the good?

185

What is the corporal for but to serve the spiritual?

186

Compassion is always ready to go to work.

187

Love is only a word until the heart is
forever open.

188

One discovers how much he loves when he
discovers how much he is willing to give and
sacrifice for other than himself.

189

The greatest friend is one who is a friend
to the world.

190

They who want only to lead haven't reached the higher state of wanting to serve.

191

The noble impulse: the sense of duty that one must give everything one has to life, that one owes this to life.

192

The more someone gives, the less he
needs, the less she needs, from others.

193

At the foundation of all great life is the
embracement of selfless commitment.

194

The reach of veritable love extends well beyond emotion.

195

The world knows nothing of love, but its beauty is enhanced the more love there is in the world.

196

If a human life is not more than just about
itself, what can it be about?

197

Is it a matter of what we want from life,
or what life wants from us?

198

The true saving of oneself is never
about oneself.

199

As long as you are here there is more
to be done, more to be learned . . .
more inner light to burn.

200

Your birth has been paid for. Your life you must pay for yourself.

201

It all comes down to the mind, the heart, the spirit, their nature and their quality — are you working on the evolution of yours . . .

202

Better than to wish others well is to
wish them spiritual growth.

203

May the highest aspirations of
humankind be achieved, and may all
strive to achieve them.

ABOUT THE AUTHOR

Carroll Blair is an author of more than twenty books and the recipient of numerous awards. His work has been well endorsed and commendably reviewed. Among his titles cited for distinction are *Through the Shadows*, winner of the Pacific Book Awards, and *Quarter Notes*, winner of the Sharp Writ Book Awards. He is an alumnus of the Boston Conservatory and lives in Massachusetts.

www.ingramcontent.com/pod-product-compliance
Lightning Source LLC
Chambersburg PA
CBHW021201020426
42331CB00003B/159